THE HUMAN RIGHT TO SOLAR ENERGY

TECHNOLOGY AT THE SERVICE OF THE PLANET

HENDERSON J. COLINA

"Our Sun is the best example that
we inhabit a prosperous world"

HENDERSON J. COLINA

With admiration and respect for all those who dedicate their daily lives to working so that solar energy can reach all

"In life, you can meet people or experience situations which will connect you to the universe and transform you forever."

Henderson C.

About the Author

HENDERSON J. COLINA (Venezuela, 1984), has dedicated himself to the public defense of Nature since he was a child. In 2001 he founded the Ecological Association for the Environmental Preservation of the state of Falcón (AEPA FALCON), which quickly became a benchmark in environmental struggle in Venezuela, supporting processes of social struggle in Latin America and other continents. Considered one of the most critical voices of Venezuelan environmentalism, he has been part of numerous global networks and alliances for environmental defense and human rights. University Studies include: Agricultural Engineering; Strategic Planning and Projects; International Cooperation; Sustainable Development; and Environmental Education. His passion for the protection of Coastal Wetlands has led him to participate in initiatives on conservation and restoration of mangrove ecosystems in various countries, achieving recognition from Embassies and Awards for Sustainable Innovation. He has lived in Philadelphia Pennsylvania, United States since 2017, where, with the support of local activists, he promotes a network for Environmental Education and Sustainability, with the aim of undertaking actions that strengthen citizen awareness.

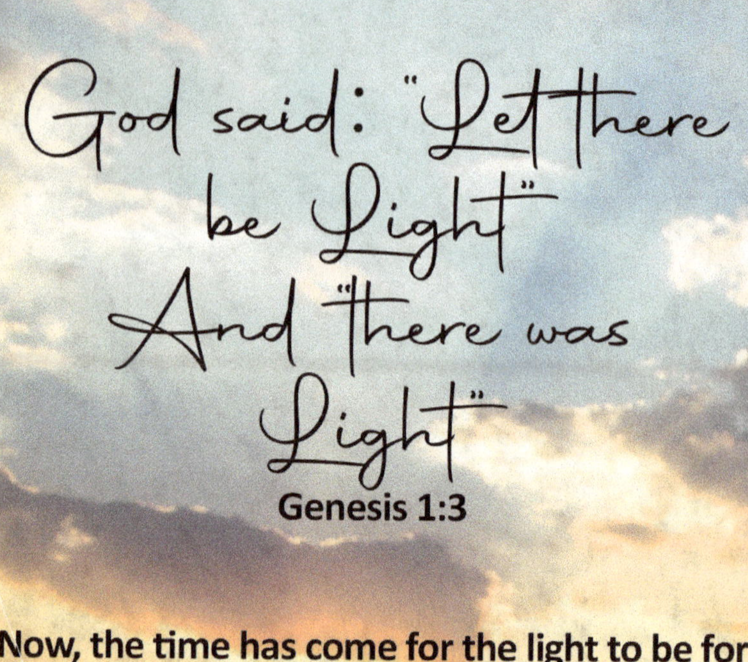

God said: "Let there be Light"
And "there was Light"
Genesis 1:3
Now, the time has come for the light to be for everyone and equally

FOREWORD

It is as if we are in a magical world, where the energy of light will always shine the way to a more kind future. Sunlight, responsible for photosynthesis, source of life, does not end with sunset or begin with sunrise on the other side of the planet. The star king never sets! In this case there would be no «day and night». This same process offers us the ecosystems that generate Blue Carbon, responsible for reducing the carbon footprint.

We have within our reach for free, a clean, renewable, sustainable source of energy. Even more striking is the fact of its availability to the people of the countries of the intertropical regions, considered poor in financial resources. It is incredible to think that the countries considered «rich» are those with less availability of Sun throughout the year.

We also allow ourselves to draw attention to that same Light as a Guiding Star, Universal Heritage, with reflections expressed in various chapters of this work. We invite the reader to learn a little more about the author, a young man who expresses with his heart and soul his thoughts and reflections towards the human right to solar energy!

Yara Schaeffer-Novelli

Senior Professor, Oceanographic Institute, University of São Paulo, Brazil

Founder of the BiomaBrasil Institute

Member of the Mangrove Specialist Group, IUCN

"The era of renewable and affordable energy for all must start today''

Antonio Guterres

General Secretary of the United Nations Organization

September 24, 2021 opening speech COP 26 on Climate Change

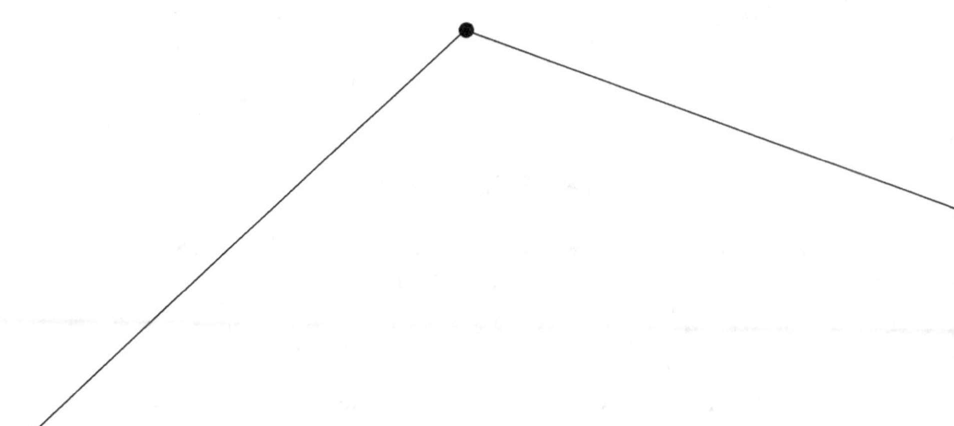

THE HUMAN RIGHT TO SOLAR ENERGY

Author

Henderson J. Colina Jimenez

Foreword

Yara Schaeffer-Novelli

Bibliographic review

Jose Amable Araujo

Graphic design

Tulio Valdelamar

Photographs

Henderson J. Colina, Tulio Valdelamar, Mariateresa Beriozka Márquez

Philadelphia, PA–United States

@Hcolinavzla @SolarHumanRight

Author's Words

When I was just 7 years old I decided that I would dedicate my whole life to the defense of Nature. Along this route I have traveled, I have compiled learning, sharing processes of struggle and resistance with many communities around the world together with social leaders who take action to defend their sustainable livelihoods, opposing the impact and destruction of those whom I will call: "carbon corporations".

In many of those struggles to which I expressed solidarity and support, I was able to witness serious violations of the most fundamental rights of human beings and the rights of Mother Earth. I live with the reality of having to say goodbye to friends because their voices were silenced. Now they are traveling in the infinite cosmos, guiding with their clarity the environmental movement that continues to fight here on Earth.

It came to the point in my home country of Venezuela where continuing this Environmental fight became a threat to the point of being jailed or killed. So, I obtained asylum in the United States. But, now the time for change has come.

This is the moment in history in which the consolidation of the era of renewable energies begins as a response to the imminent climate crisis and the imperative need to achieve global peace in the face of innumerable wars that are always defined by the geopolitics of natural resources and energy sources.

An era that is led by the Solar Energy sector as a sustainable, low-energy source, and easy to install. A sector that generates numerous jobs capable of strengthening the economy and what is most important for Humanity: "it is the energy source capable of quickly and effectively reducing the carbon footprint".

For this reason, I would like to congratulate all those who work day-by-day in the solar energy sector, for their efforts, their dedication, their technological innovations and their leadership to rapidly grow a new global service provision network that leads to independence energy. I will call all of them "warriors of light". The world is witnessing and participating in what you do for all of us, we are witnesses of your perseverance, recognizing that your work transforms into well-being for the planet and marks the beginning of a new era; The Solar Age.

INDEX

CHAPTER I: THE SUN, SOURCE OF UNIVERSAL LIFE.16

CHAPTER II: THE RENEWING ENERGIES OF LIFE......21

CHAPTER III: SOLAR COMPANIES, A SECTOR COMMITTED TO THE PLANET...................................... 30

7 REASONS TO BE SOLAR...................................*43*

CHAPTER IV: SOLAR ENERGY, A SOURCE OF SUSTAINABLE EMPLOYMENT.......................................45

CHAPTER V: SOLAR ENERGY AS A HUMAN RIGHT.....54

CHAPTER VI: ENVIRONMENTAL EDUCATION, KEY TO PROMOTE SOLAR ENERGY...65

THE 4 GOALS OF ENVIRONMENTAL EDUCATION FOR SOLAR ENERGY...*68*

REFERENCES...73

"Solar energy is more than an inexhaustible and affordable source. It is, without a doubt, a Universal Heritage that gives us the opportunity for energy independence from homes, leaving a mark of light in this generation"

Henderson Colina

The sun, source of universal life

An important part of the first designs for children include images related to the Sun. When I participate in environmental education sessions in schools and communities, I can feel the creative force, their energy and how children manifest dreams in what only adults would see as a doodle on a paper sheet. The children manifest with the dynamic, stories and art that "the sun is present at all times".

If only we listened to the clarity and honesty of children, our climate summits would not be global meetings in the "desperate search" to achieve a "binding climate agreement". Science has managed to show data that should lead us to develop structural changes in the system.

It should be clear that, without a doubt, it is climate change and its consequences that will push us to the state of consciousness that we so much need to achieve. We are witnesses how this new generation, mostly young, has formed the leaders of the present, not of the future. Leaders who are now building social processes for a common future with new approaches, paradigms and ideas of diversity and inclusion.

All of them working with love and dedication in companies, governments, associations, volunteer groups, interconnected with each other, many still without having noticed that they are part of a new social fabric.

After the Millennium Declaration: September 2000, the United Nations (UN) began to promote a global agenda for common goals. At that time, solar energy was still seen as an alternative to combat poverty and guarantee access to electricity in rural communities.

In August 2001, I had the opportunity to participate as a volunteer in a Renewable Energy program for the economically depressed areas of the Falconian semi-arid region, in the Northwest of Venezuela, in South America. An initiative promoted by the Andean Development Corporation (CAF) we were in a rural settlement that seemed like an inhospitable place.

The aridity of the landscape showed a desert without potential when seen through the magnifying glass of a city dweller, but I was surprised when I heard this premise from one of the technology experts who accompanied us: "it seems that there is nothing here, but, with all the solar energy that this place generates, we could illuminate a good part of New York City. I did not understand what relationship that yellow landscape of xerophytic plants had with a place as modern as the Big Apple. It seemed crazy, but the visionary nature of the message planted a seed of awareness and concern in all the attendees.

The truth is that we were looking for "energy alternatives" for this population, because the high costs of power lines make new electrical projects in rural agricultural communities unfeasible. We see then, how the little planning and the null application of technologies according to those spaces takes precedence over the most basic rights of the people. I remember during the introductory talk by experts in renewable energies from the "Francisco de Miranda" University that "guaranteeing the population access to energy is a human rights issue."

We all knew that under our feet millions of barrels of oil and gas were present. Also large reserves of underground water and a relentless sun that we could take advantage of in a sustainable way in those spaces. However, in Venezuela, a country so rich in natural resources, biodiversity and culture, it was not explained why a good part of the population did not have access to something as fundamental as energy, so it is necessary. Despite this, the existence of trials by previous governments that began to develop a solar plant to take advantage of that incidence of light in that space were later abandoned. While at the same time, in public discourse we all hear that "the blame for the environmental disaster lies with the richest countries, the most powerful, and the great powers that plunder nature for their greed."

Populism! We are still hearing this discourse around climate change summits and conferences, it seems that the simple solution is to blame others for the problem to avoid taking responsibility because, I think I have seen more greed in the global south than in developed countries that I have visited, for example, mining in my country Venezuela is destroying the Amazon, creating new deserts.

In my opinion, in many countries of the Global North, people focus on their own social dynamics and many even voluntarily help people and associations in countries where poverty is the prevailing effect of corruption and weak democracies. Although I must ascertain that not everything is perfect, since there is inequality in these countries as in all the others, there are agendas and issues to attend to.

Climate Change is a global issue and we are all generating pollution due to the civilizational pattern that dominates the system, so the North-South debate has lost validity. The climate crisis is affecting everyone equally and we must resolve it together on a common agenda. The reality has been showing different things, that political discourse of the 80's is expiring. While many are exhausted in the ideological debate in many countries around the planet there are companies and citizens who are promoting the change from carbon energies towards renewable energies.

It is also true that the impulse of some political sectors is needed, including that of those who only waste their strength in pure criticism without offering genuine contributions.

For decades, carbon corporations dedicated their technology and labor to the generation of energy resources for large cities, creating the fantasy of being inexhaustible, sustainable sources capable of satisfying the unbridled consumption of unconsciousness - the same one that plunged us into the current climate crisis.

However, every crisis opens the door to new opportunities, which is why it is time for renewable energies and all the range of options, including solar energy, which has the necessary characteristics to be the renewable energy that helps us to quickly reduce the carbon footprint.

Humanity throughout its evolutionary process has documented its link with the elements of nature, showing vital links that are still in force. We see this clearly in the images of the caves that date from the so-called Stone Age, temples and the network of pyramids around the world. All ancient cultures appreciated the sun not only observed as a symbol of worship, but also as a source of prosperity and abundance.

At this time, it seems that this solar principle remains the same, only which by adding technological innovations, we managed to encapsulate all the knowledge in small devices that are easy to move and all the facilities that modernity offers. I refer to those instruments or equipment which are called photovoltaic panels.

In 1839 when scientist Alexander Edmond Becquerel published his first paper on the effects of temperature on the duration of phosphorescent light emission, the world was skeptical. Then, in 1883, American inventor Charles Fritz created the first working selenium solar cell.

Years later, in 1905 Albert Einstein proposed a new quantum theory of light and explained the photoelectric effect in a landmark paper for which he received the Nobel Prize in Physics in 1921. It was undoubtedly at this time that the momentum for the Solar subject began, from the added value that Einstein's reputation gave, appreciated were the efforts of all those other scientists who were pioneers. Later, what is known as the breakthrough towards solar cells, in 1954 following the work of Bell Laboratories, Daryl Chapin, Calvin Fuller, and Gerald Pearson, created a more practical solar cell using silicon.

At the time when these technological innovations were presented, it is possible that many of us could not imagine where they would end up, in fact, it has not ended. The solar energy sector continues to present constant innovations now at the hands of such important global corporations as Tesla, which presents us with devices to store energy generated in solar panels and new photovoltaic systems such as solar tiles, which gives added value to the model of sustainable architecture and urban landscaping.

Now, in 1979, a historical event set the tone for the new reality: the rise in price and scarcity of oil, which made the reality of the United States' dependence on these foreign energy resources obvious. At this time, President Jimmy Carter had solar panels installed on the roof of the White House, thus making solar energy more tangible to the people, thereby disseminating knowledge about it to the present.

This gesture by President Jimmy Carter marked the beginning of a new path in the energy policy of the United States, one of the great global powers; and it is partly responsible for all the positive changes and transformations that we see materialized today.

All this evolution of solar energy has been, in large part, the effect of scientific contributions and the commitment of visionary entrepreneurs, who with their day-to-day work have created the conditions for "the solar revolution", which has had exponential growth, especially in the photovoltaic sector, representing the easiest renewable energy to install and expand around the planet.

The renewing energies of life

When we talk about renewable energy, clean energy or sustainable livelihoods, we are referring primarily to the way we conceive life, our interactions with nature and the consequences that derive from these relationships. So, the first thing we must recognize is that Life has been present not only since the existence of our human ancestors, but millions of years ago, so the planet has managed without us, let's stop believing those lies that we are going to save the world.

We are part of a whole, of an ecosystem that is constantly evolving. Consequently, the environmental crisis is nothing more than the reflection of all forms of violence between humans and with the rest of the other forms of life on the planet.

Personally, there was a time when I was very concerned about how reactions from expressing my environmentalist ideas, my way of perceiving life, the universe, the cosmos, and human relationships would resonate in others. So, I was able to understand that this is part of people's beliefs, values and religiosity. As an example: we were raised in a system where we are made to believe that "you must suffer to be happy", "One day it will happen, one day", "after ecosystems are destroyed, many will learn to value them". Without a doubt it is impossible to obtain changes if we practice repetitive schemes.

This is the result of the educational system, the ways in which the world was organized and how society was formed, but now we are in the era of knowledge and communication. This quantum leap leaves us in the midst of changes that respond to human nature: Innovation. And despite the fact that any change will create resistance, when something dies or is transformed to give way to another life, the forces that are unleashed employ the use of a lot of energy.

This is what is happening in this great transition towards renewable energies. There is uncertainty, doubts, perhaps even distrust but we must expand our minds and recognize that we are in a new era.

A decisive moment for a world of finite natural resources- very well expressed in the studies of the limits of growth- and, although it is possible that many do not believe, this is happening because life, like a river on a mountain path, seeks a way, forges the path. In this way we know that life will prevail with or without us. Of course, it would be good, in addition to demonstrating our real intelligence, to be on the right side.

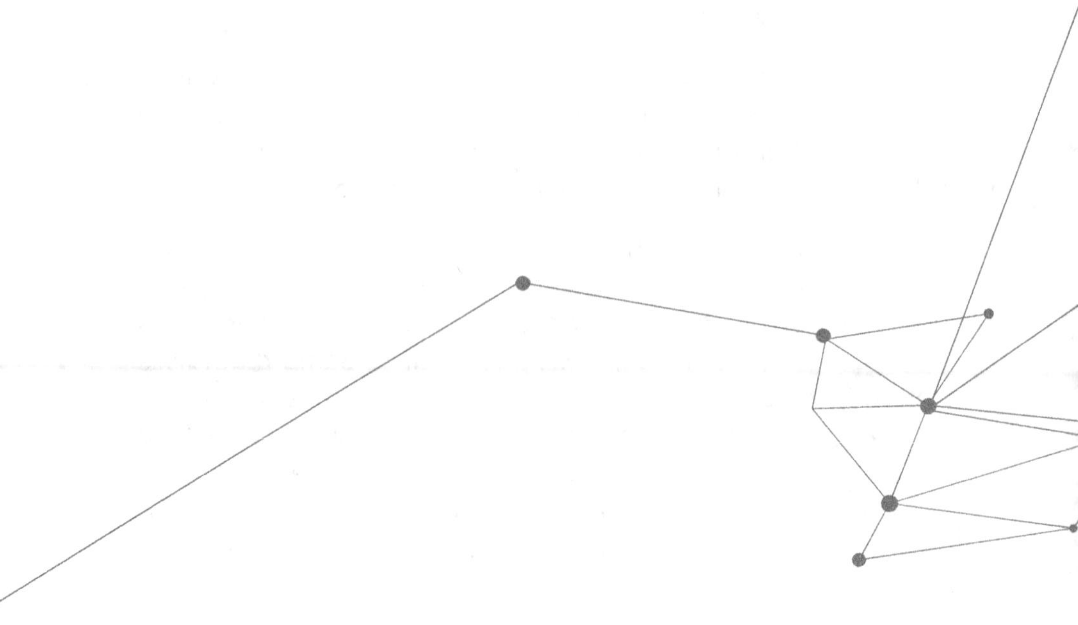

Planet Earth is alive! It is not just an inanimate body made up of rock and water that we use as a home

James Lovelock

Many times you also may have asked yourself questions such as: What is Life? And those many things to which we seek answers and that are sometimes part of the debate with that people with whom we feel good: friends, co-workers, that stranger we met on a trip. If you have asked yourself this, I am so happy that you can be reading my book, since the perception we have about Life impacts everything we are and project around us.

Now, what does all this about Life has to do with renewable energy? To understand this, it is necessary to analyze some of the theories underlying the evolution of Life. It is no coincidence that the best known theory of Evolution is the Natural Selection of Species in which Charles Darwin states that: "Because resources are limited in nature, organisms with heritable traits that favor survival and reproduction, they will tend to leave more offspring than their peers, which causes the frequency of these characteristics to increase over several generations." Taking these premises, for 20 years I have dedicated myself to the study of biology and its applicability to the social sciences.

In almost all environmental conflict processes I have heard things like: companies and governments are stronger and more powerful! The mega-project is going to be carried out because the community is weak against them! Behind that war, what is there is interest in such natural resources! This is nothing more than the effect of a wrong interpretation of natural selection applied to social behavior.

This scheme of unbridled competition for power, winning, standing out, unlimited wealth accumulation, social inequality, this is getting us nowhere. However, I am respectful of the way many interpret life. Social Darwinism is perhaps present in some elements of our daily lives, but as a human species, we must be careful about what kind of offspring we want to leave and what conditions the planet will be in for our future generations and the rest of all life forms.

I highly value the knowledge and contributions of all scientists. This is as important as the grain of pollen that travels, moved by the wind, to pollinate another flower.

As fundamental as the interaction between microorganisms that regulate key biological processes for the sustainability of the planet. Transcendental like the nuptial flight of ephemeral insects once the rain has passed because I see that as Life and we are part of it. It is not our property. Everything is interconnected. We are all interrelated.

Darwin left us a valuable contribution. In a certain sense his Natural Selection has logical explanations, but it is possible that we interpret it in a wrong way: the world, life, society, is more than a permanent competition and a fight for limited resources, or the survival of the fittest or the strongest.

There are other theories that propose relationships other than competition as an evolutionary mechanism, on the understanding that we recognize that Sustainability is cooperation, harmony, respect, balance, synergy and these values are also part of Life, expressing itself in various ways. Symbiogenesis is the theory of evolution presented by the expert in Microbiology Lynn Margulis from the University of Massachusetts.

The theory contains a high technical value and I highly recommend reading it in more detail. In her theory, Margulis tells us, among many things, how "the most primitive forms of life established relationships of serial symbiotic cooperation to shape the life we know today"... "two organisms that have evolved separately are associated in a certain moment, their association is beneficial in the environment in which they live and finally they end up being a single organism" the professor based her studies on the analysis of microorganisms and their interactions.

In many of her books, which she published together with Dorion Sagan, her son and unconditional ally, Lynn Margulis invites us to reflect on the various independent processes of the planet as a biological organism where most of its interactions are based on symbiotic dynamics, allowing Life as a whole to continue its process, in which human beings are only a part of this evolutionary process. My admiration for Lynn Margulis goes beyond the deep respect for the high scientific value.

Those of us who have stopped to learn about her story know that her career was not entirely easy. The professor persevered a lot so that her scientific work was accepted and published. Not only because her work challenged the prevailing evolutionary theory at the time and which was considered the only way to explain the origin of Life, but also because she was a woman, because she was critical, because of her innovative style that challenged the established paradigms. Undoubtedly, Margulis was a precursor.

On many occasions I have believed that at a global level, the summary of Lynn Margulis' theory should be in the educational program of all countries. It should even be at the entrance of the headquarters of all those International organizations that say they work for World Peace, for Sustainability, for The Planet, because it is perhaps the most valuable scientific contribution of this century.

It is the philosophical root of the renewable, of what we have called "alternative", that which is possible, that other world, that model which it simply does not oppose, it manifests itself. It presents itself and tells us here I am present, I am Life itself, what are you doing with everything I have created over millions of years of evolution? Symbiogenesis starts from the acceptance of the diversity of all forms of life. It is an exciting theory that serves as scientific support for the proposal of the cooperative against the scheme of domination of the human over the human and the rest of the present biological forms.

The Sun, all forms of energy, the cycles and processes that derive from it, are a reflection of a scheme of coexistence in universal harmony to facilitate optimal conditions of durability in time and space.

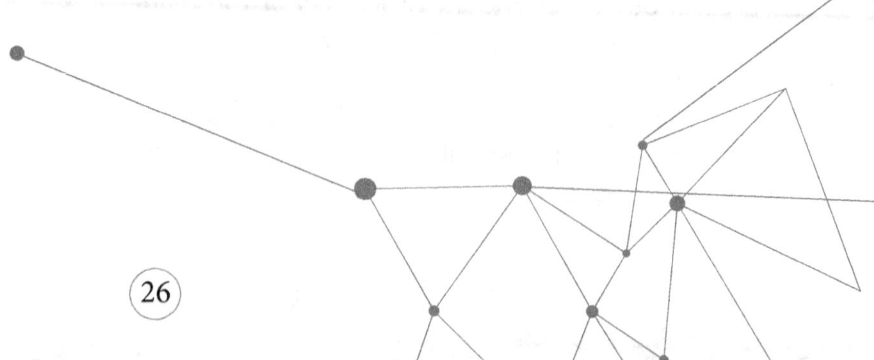

*We can reflect that
the carbon footprint is a
reflection of an erroneous
development model where
the excessive exploitation of
Nature, including the human
species, has been imposed as
a social criterion and where
the commodification of Life
is the prevailing premise*

Henderson Colina

We must then understand that, for life to continue its continuous evolution, it is important to reflect on what type of relationships will prevail. Under this premise, the Sun is not only a source of energy for human well-being, it is a universal heritage that drives biological processes on Earth and regulates various natural cycles.

That is why for the peoples of the world, the sun and the energy derived from it is by natural order a right that we acquire with life. All of this is interconnected with each other with the various elements with which we have achieved, being recognized as principles inherent to humanity, the right to water, the right to land, the right to clean air, now It's time to recognize the right to solar energy.

In short, to make way for new forms of energy and broaden the focus on sustainability, we must understand that the principle of competition as the predominant pattern for the durability of some forms of life over others and on which the model of world development and the civilizational pattern is no longer the only approach to the study of the origin of life and its development. We have to cooperate, work in synergy, this will facilitate the quantum leap that global society needs and we are building in a state of higher consciousness.

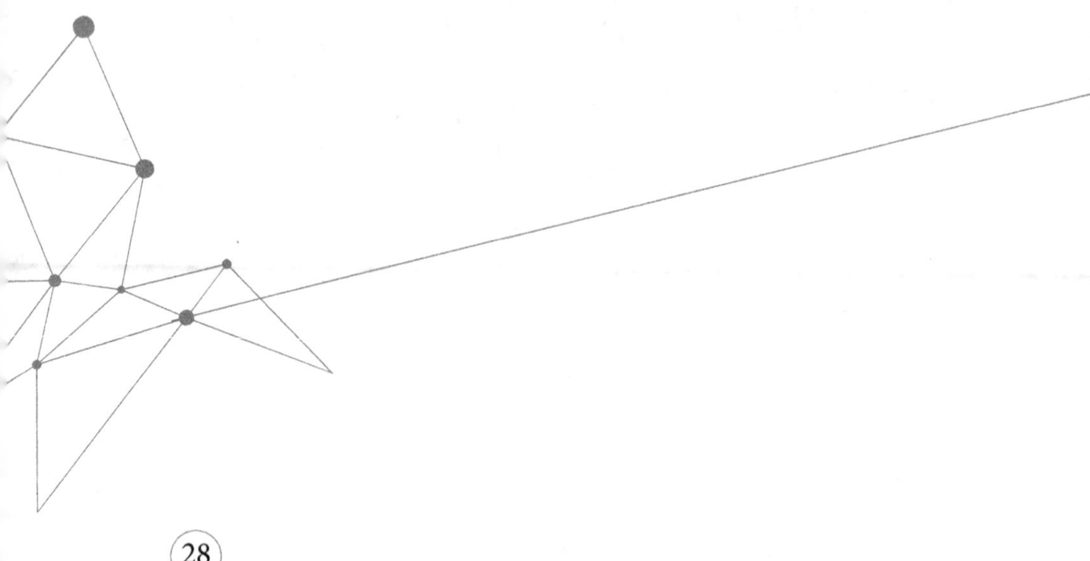

"Life is a symbiotic and cooperative union that allows those who associate to succeed"
Lynn Margulis
University of Massachusetts

Solar companies, a sector committed to the planet

For nearly 20 years I have studied the dynamics of companies and the environment of which they are part. I remember the triangulation that we learned in Higher Education Centers and so many training days in various countries "companies, society and environment", to that They incorporated the concept of Governments or State, later they said: we must add the International organizations, you know, important decisions are made there.

But, the first thing we must understand is that companies, as an associative body, are made up of people, individuals who respond to a social dynamic, who are living beings, who choose their rulers and, without a doubt, who will be impacted by the decisions made in World Organizations. Then I felt that they were making something so simple very complex.

At first, I saw how companies did not feel so comfortable with environmental movements. They saw us as enemies. In fact, many continue to see us as adversaries. We people who oppose "development", but, of course, if we oppose voracious developmentalism, we love life, how are we going to support so much destruction? Especially the impacts of carbon corporations. I grew up seeing how Oil and its derivatives stained the coasts of the beaches and seas of the beautiful place where I was born, and people saw it as normal.

Even the artisanal fishermen said that "oil spills are a job opportunity, since the company hired me to clean the beaches." They are those things that one should stop to think and reflect upon. Undoubtedly, ignorance makes us so dangerous, not only for the planet, but with ourselves.

Throughout this process of social resistance, strong criticism and opposition campaigns to carbon corporations, global society has witnessed how the persecution and murder of environmental leaders has increased exponentially. This has always happened. Only since the advancement in communications has information become global and thanks to organizations such as Global Witness, this problem has become visible and we have managed to make the population aware of these issues.

There were times I was scared. It's normal. I'm human. Once, in the middle of a press conference where even international media correspondents were present, a journalist asked me, "what is behind all of this that you do, do you expose yourself like this? Have you ever felt fear for your life and your colleagues' lives?" I was not used to those types of questions, they always asked me questions related to environmental impacts, laws, and those very common things.

Then there was a silence in the whole room that was interrupted with a "yes, I'm scared, sometimes my hands get sweaty, I'm human, but you know what? I believe and am convinced that we must overcome together that fear with which we were born and that we were taught for generations. That is the root of all this environmental disaster" perhaps until that moment I did not know how much we had come to influence public policies and touch interests that made the danger visible.

So I started new studies, this time in international law, development cooperation, and conflict management. Those companies that I had opposed began to see a renewed discourse. I no longer protested outside, I was sitting there with the managers debating, telling them things up front.

Some started social responsibility programs, others radicalized their policies, others completely ignored us, at least we thought so, but later we found out that they even recorded our interviews on radio and television and their lawyers analyzed them looking for legal resources to incriminate us. Practices that many carbon corporations continue practicing around the world.

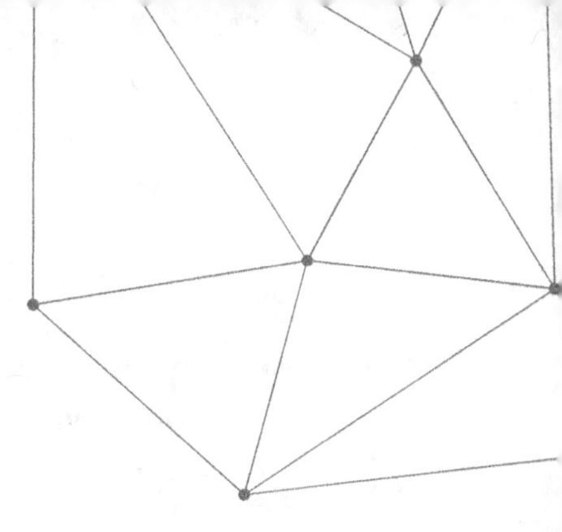

> *"Every action, however small it may seem, generates changes"*
>
> **Julia Butterfly Hill**

I believe that the philosophy of the environmental movement is undergoing a significant change. This new great transition to renewable energies is unstoppable. It will not only reduce the carbon footprint, it will also open the way to reduce the strong pressures on environmental leaders and activists who, due to their strong public advocacy campaigns, face serious threats and persecution.

The success of renewable energy companies, in part, will be based on reflecting on the lessons learned that have been derived from the senescent "Carbon Era". There will be strong opposition, they will say things like, "there is no capacity to sustain the current development model." Though, we must continue in the natural dynamics of life while many wear themselves out in the ideological debate of pointing out those responsible for climate change.

Interesting things are happening around the planet that motivate us, inspire us, make us passionate to continue fighting, and the relationship of many companies with the environment with which they interact is changing. Now we can talk about companies where the environmental philosophy is present in all their processes. That is an important corporate value.

Now when we fly over the territory, we not only see the environmental impacts; deforestation, the large chimneys of carbon corporations, we are seeing how renewable energy is gaining space. It is a reality. We are progressively reducing the carbon footprint. The sun is out. The wind is blowing in our favor. We must be more optimistic as we continue to demand greater changes while acknowledging progress. We are winning, we are cooperating for the common good.

During the development of this research, I remember reading about 200 interviews with leaders of various renewable energy companies and influential personalities around the world of sustainability. As you can imagine I spent hours working. Then Life sent a person who showed me the route and gave words of encouragement and inspiration. He spoke to me about a particular sector- solar companies - so I focused on analyzing what was happening in this area.

The exponential growth of its actions in the stock market. The expansion of the networks of companies that install solar panels The conversion of many homes to sustainable houses. That's how I found, after deep reading, something that brought me closer to dawn. Among them, an interview that on August 5th, 2021, the New York Times conducted with North American renewable energy market expert Mary Powell, who has an entire career dedicated to research and development in green energies, the sum of a business life corporative and altruistic approach, benchmarks of leadership of what I will call "green corporations".

It is very comforting for a young man like me who has dedicated his life to defending Nature, to hear from senior managers who are passionate about leading alternatives to stop climate change. I am not surprised that again, as happened with Lynn Margulis, it is women who I see being pioneers. These are the people we need to consolidate the unstoppable solar age.

It makes me extremely happy to see how around the world, many environmental leaders and sensitive people to Nature are promoting changes from the private sector. It is interesting to see how there is a social contract between communities and companies. In particular, this new trend of sustainable companies.

In most companies that I had the opportunity to study, more than 60% of the entire network of workers are young. This is perhaps one of the reasons why there has been such an exponential growth in the solar sector.

The youth force added to the experience of qualified experts, technologists and people with a lot of experience in the business and marketing area are generating positive figures, good indicators of development.

"My passion for climate change is the reason why I am passionate about this company"

Mary Powell, CEO of Sunrun

It is important to recognize how the association of the technology giant TESLA with solar energy companies not only guarantees the advancement and expansion of the photovoltaic sector in the world, but it will also allow the association of this energy source with others such as hydrogen. Once again we see how cooperation and synergy are expressed in the foundation of evolution. On this occasion, a technological evolution.

The message of the recent Conference of the Parties on Climate Change (COP 26) held in Glasgow, in the United Kingdom, is clear to us, "the way to reduce the carbon footprint is, among other things, to support the expansion of renewable energies and, of all these, solar energy has the appropriate characteristics for this purpose in addition to being a sector that generates numerous jobs, social investment and facilitates mechanisms to raise awareness among the population in general", words of Antonio Guterres himself, Secretary General of the United Nations Organization.

Within all of this, technological innovation will play a fundamental role. Likewise, the adaptation of many legal norms in the different countries is necessary. We see progress and important announcements by governments, however, political will is required from all sectors including their sworn duty to be socially responsible and active implementation of solutions to reduce the impacts of climate change.

It is not just needed from companies, environmental associations and some government initiatives, but also active participation by the scientific community is needed. Not only to predict the impacts, i.e. disasters, but also to develop the renewable energy sector by making forecasts, impact analysis, reducing emissions in .the process, and having coherence between the speech and reality. It's simple. Only, once again we must work in synergy.

The international discourse of the regionalization of the world loses force from the traditional ideological dimension when the space station or NASA show us images of the planet. There we only see a single world.

There the language, the political systems and the borders of the countries cannot be distinguished. In this new era, solar energy is a living example of globalization, in this new era the sun rises for everyone.

I strongly believe in the private sector. Companies. Entrepreneurs. Many companies in the renewable energy sector are led by managers who have implemented the sustainable development goals that the United Nations has proposed in the global spirit of sustainability.

Currently, companies create associations and invest in the social sector and science and technology. Many specific actions add up to great global contributions for collective well-being. For decades, we have lived in the institution of human rights, which is not bad, but which has created a lot of bureaucracy, processes, protocols which elevate simple debates to legally complex scenarios, world summits, and large conferences, among others.

One of the specific responses to climate change lies in companies and society. That is, committed service providers and citizens who raise awareness by seeing concrete and real results. It's as simple as this: Once families manage to install their solar system at home, the consumption of energy from carbon decreases, then atmospheric emissions are reduced. It is cheap energy, clean energy, a sector that generates numerous jobs and it is possible, as it is already happening. The energy generated from solar sources exceeds consumption and also contributes energy to the conventional network.

This has already been reported in certain regions of Australia, for example. Now in a new stage, the recognition of solar energy as a human right of the peoples of the world will be fundamental. This will allow the governments of the planet to promote or assume greater investment in the solar sector. This will create greater possibilities and will allow greater sources of employment at a time when the global economy needs to be strengthened by the effects of the most recent pandemic. Similarly, it is a step towards the legal recognition of something that represents a world heritage.

"If you wanted the United States to run solely on solar energy, you would simply need a small corner of Nevada, Texas or Utah; it would only take 100 x 100 square miles of solar panels to power the entire United States. The batteries you would need to store the energy, so you have electricity 24/7, would be 1 per 1 mile."

Elon Musk

Tesla CEO, At the NGA Summer Meeting, 2017

The proposals of the Tesla Corporation have the world with great hope. The most interesting thing in all this, is that we know that a high content of innovation accompanies all the actions that the young entrepreneur Elon Musk promotes. The solar energy sector not only needs investment, it requires that Science and Technology get to work to guarantee improvements throughout the value chain under the premise that it is not enough to do it well.

There will always be new ways to make it better, that is, quality principles. A tangible example is the proposal for solar roof, where roofs and photovoltaic sheets are presented that add value to construction and architecture methods for large-scale sustainable projects. We have begun to incorporate family units into the criteria of sustainable houses.

Now we must point towards ecological cities, What seemed like a utopia is a reality. As well as the viability of solar cars. We see that Tesla has awakened creativity, hope and good news. So necessary in the midst is the need for new leadership approaches. Let us remember that less than a decade ago, the world questioned the possibility of electric cars. Now, in many countries there are solar cars, with Tesla being the leader in the sector.

I am fully confident that Tesla's contributions will serve to speed up the Solar Age, facilitate installation, maintenance, the potential of the panel network, the integration of new materials and the reduction of the ecological footprint in any of the processes related to solar panels. They will help not only to reduce the consumption of conventional energy, but they will also allow the incorporation of clean energy to the distribution network already established in the various cities around the planet.

One of the things that excites me the most is knowing that solar energy will return with force to the areas for which it was initially proposed as an alternative: rural areas and agricultural areas. We will be able to enjoy seeing how in the 21st century there are communities that they will say for the first time there was light! This is social justice, energy justice, this is equality, this is opportunities for all, and it is a human rights issue without a doubt.

Based on the studies on solar energy, I have proposed the Declaration of Principles entitled 7 reasons to be solar, in it, the general public will be able to have summarized information about the promise of the solar sector with the objective of its easy understanding and pedagogical strategy, to the purposes of gaining allies for the sector.

The criteria that support the 7 reasons add the social, economic and environmental dimensions, to which Science and Technology with a Human Rights approach are incorporated.

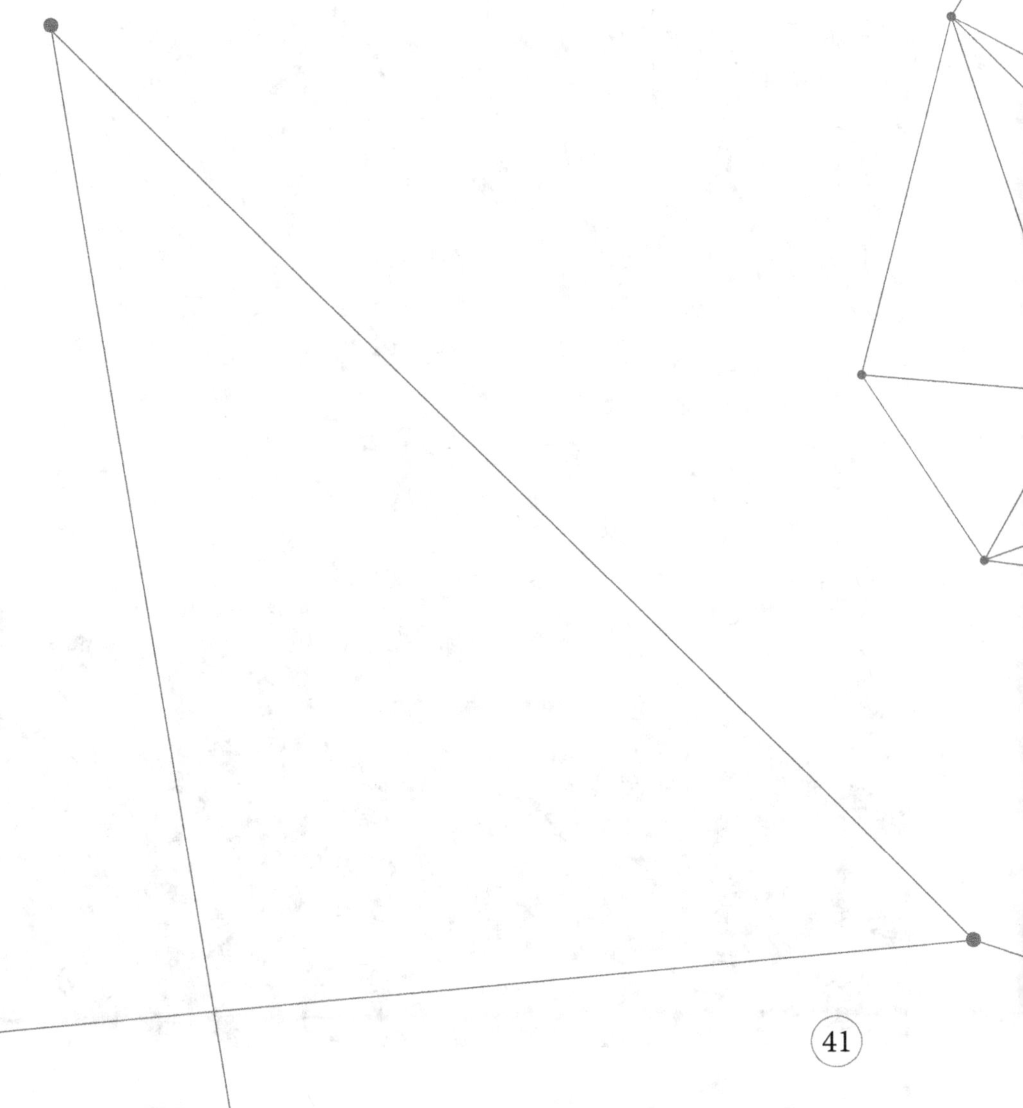

"Cleaning up the environment doesn't have to mean sacrifice. Clean energy is abundant and we have the necessary tools to take advantage of it. So that pollution, scarcity and uncertainty become things of the past".

Mary Powell
CEO of Sunrun

7 reasons why solar energy can and should be universal:

1. It does not pollute

Photovoltaic solar energy does not emit toxic substances or pollutants into the air, within the production chains, environmental impacts are reduced to a minimum

2. It helps to restrain climate change

Photovoltaic solar energy does not emit greenhouse gases. A solar panel system installed on a rooftop can reduce the pollution of 100 tons of carbon dioxide.

3. It is cheaper

Solar energy, especially photovoltaic, is cheaper than conventional energies in almost the entire world; which makes them competitive compared to conventional ones, and accessible to all populations.

4. It is inexhaustible

Although solar photovoltaic systems can have a useful life of up to 35 years, their source, which is the energy of the sun, is unlimited, it is found all over the world and it adapts to different natural cycles. Unlike conventional energy sources like coal, gas, oil and nuclear power.

5. It generates employment and autonomy

Being available throughout the planet does not generate dependence on a few companies, or large economic powers. It reduces energy imports and generates employment locally. One more point in favor of sustainable development.

6. Easy Installation

Its technology allows access to all, it is affordable and easily accessible, and its installation is simple by technicians from specialized companies.

7. Global reach

It is available throughout the planet, so it becomes the best way to provide electricity to isolated places where installing power lines is expensive and in urban areas where high energy consumption is concentrated.

"Photovoltaic energy is perhaps the most popular and fastest growing sector of solar technology"

Rhone Resch

The Solar Energy Industries Association (SEIA) USA

Solar energy source of sustainable employment

Photovoltaic solar energy has led the field of renewable energies, representing some 4 million jobs today. Large-scale solar installations feed into grid power, while smaller off-grid solar installations offer much-needed electricity access to remote and energy-poor communities. Worldwide, solar PV added 127 GW of new capacity in 2020, up from 98 GW in 2019. Asia showed a significant increase, mainly in five countries (China, Vietnam, India, Republic of Korea and Japan). Europe installed 20.8 GW, the United States another 15 GW, Australia 4.4 GW and Brazil 3.3 GW.

The main sources of employment within renewable energies are wind and photovoltaic. From wind energy we have seen since September 2020. The New Jersey Economic Development Authority in the United States decided to provide 4.5 USD million to support the development of a workforce in renewable wind energy through the Clean Energy Program. Also in New York, the State University of New York and the Energy Research and Development Authority (NYSERDA) launched the new State Institute for Training in Offshore Wind Energy with which they hope to train more than 2,500 workers.

From both scenarios, photovoltaic solar energy continues to be the greatest driver of employment and growth in the renewable energy sector. In the 1.5°C temperature rise scenario, around 20 million jobs can be created by 2050, especially for solar energy, of which 77% will be in photovoltaic energy, 15% produced by solar heaters (CSA) and 8% in by concentrating solar energy.

The current investment in solar energy exceeds the rest of the renewable energies. From this it is very positively derived that photovoltaic energy requires a workforce to be able to be installed and distribute the energy, generating numerous jobs and economic prosperity.

The benefits and advantages of renewable energies such as solar include not only the reduction of carbon in the atmosphere and reduction of air pollution, but also include a series of socioeconomic benefits that are currently having a significant impact. This It is the product of the decrease in the costs of implementing solar energy and the advancement of technologies, together with the implementation of government policies in support of renewable energy.

The health benefits offered by solar energy are in its ability to be a clean energy that does not pollute the environment. Currently, solar energy can be implemented in a modular way and from there can be distributed it in your home, making it less prone to failures in the scaling of this technology. This advantage allows this technology to be easily implemented during climate change events and environmental emergencies providing electricity without the need for complex infrastructure for it. Thus, avoiding catastrophic events such as what happened in the state of Texas, United States in 2020 or other unexpected situations that derive from the current climate crisis.

Data on annual employment by renewable energy shows that 8.1 million people worldwide, excluding hydroelectric, work in "Energies" increasing at a rate of 5% per year since 2015. When comparing this with other sectors the Total number of renewable energy jobs continue to rise in stark contrast to other depressed labor markets in the energy sector.

But what encourages us even more is that the greatest growth comes from photovoltaic solar energy, which is considered the largest employer sector within renewable energies with 2.8 million jobs and jobs worldwide, with a rate growth of 11%. Today it continues to grow consistently in the United States and Japan. For experts in the area, world GDP can increase considerably if the production of renewable energy is doubled. Especially, since this would save trillions of dollars equivalent in pollution impacts.

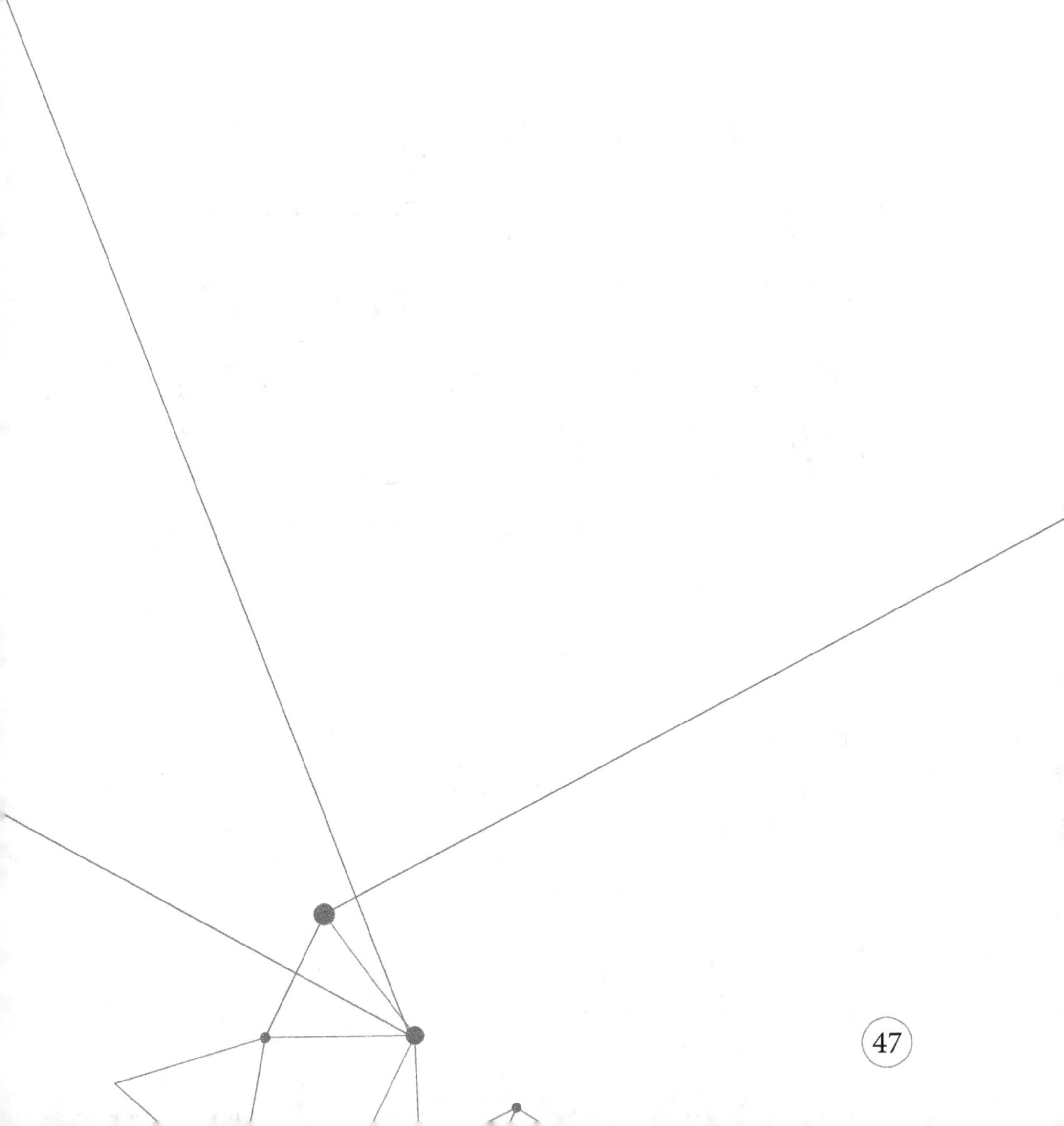

"Solar energy is the cheapest energy source in most countries and generates more jobs than the fossil fuel sector"

Antonio Guterres, United Nations COP 26 Climate Change

In addition, being a new business management model, most renewable energy corporations integrate the gender and diversity approach. This is another important achievement that I could see by analyzing the various communications, press releases, managers' speeches and content analysis in the various social networks of numerous corporations. Ensuring a work environment in accordance with the principles of sustainability makes the solar energy sector attractive, as well as promoting the happiness of its workers.

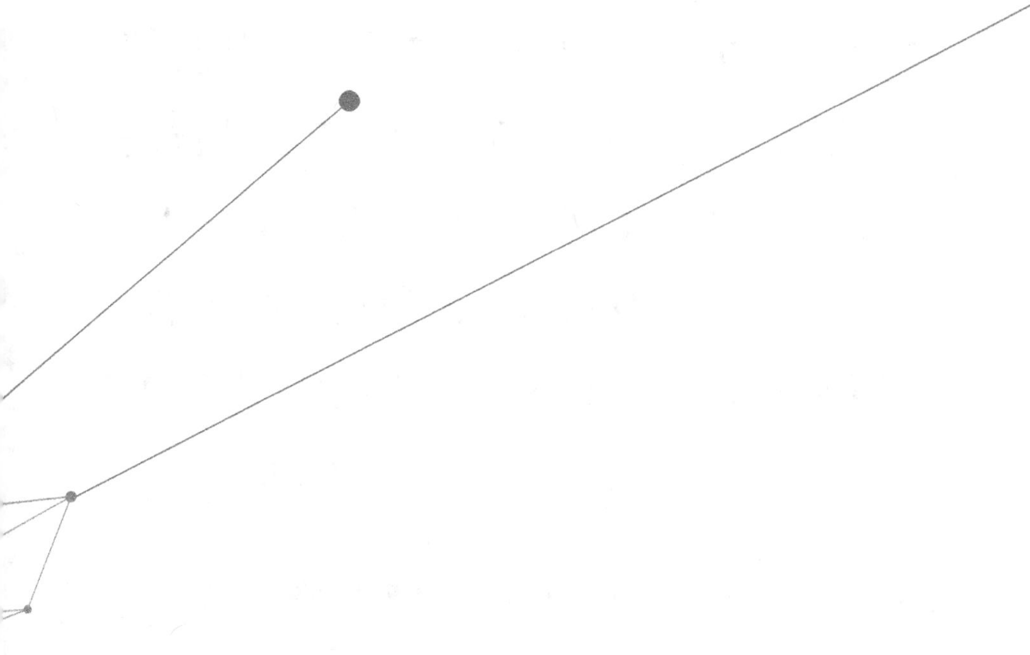

"Investing in clean and affordable energy for all will improve the well-being of billions of people. It can create the green jobs that we urgently need for the recovery from the COVID-19 crisis. It will promote all the Sustainable Development Goals. And it is the most important solution to avoid a climate catastrophe"

Antonio Guterres

Secretary General of the United Nations

SOLAR ENERGY

ENVIRONMENTAL WELL-BEING
(Reduction of polluting emissions, low carbon footprint)

SOCIAL WELFARE
(strengthening awareness in the community, investment in science and technology)

ECONOMIC WELFARE
(potential job creation, public and private investment)

Currently, we see a strong commitment from global organizations to consider promoting greater investment in renewable energy. Even when a consensus is not achieved by all countries, most of them are betting on photovoltaic solar energy as a new form of production for energy independence, especially due to the impact that dependence on oil has on economies.

Furthermore, the territorial conflicts that have been triggered throughout the history of humanity by the urgent need for access to this limited resource. Even the oil-producing countries, most of which are not so receptive to this new world trend, will benefit from the promotion of renewable energies. They will be able to reduce the historical environmental liabilities associated with the oil industry, promoting sustainable tourism and other forms of more endogenous economy.

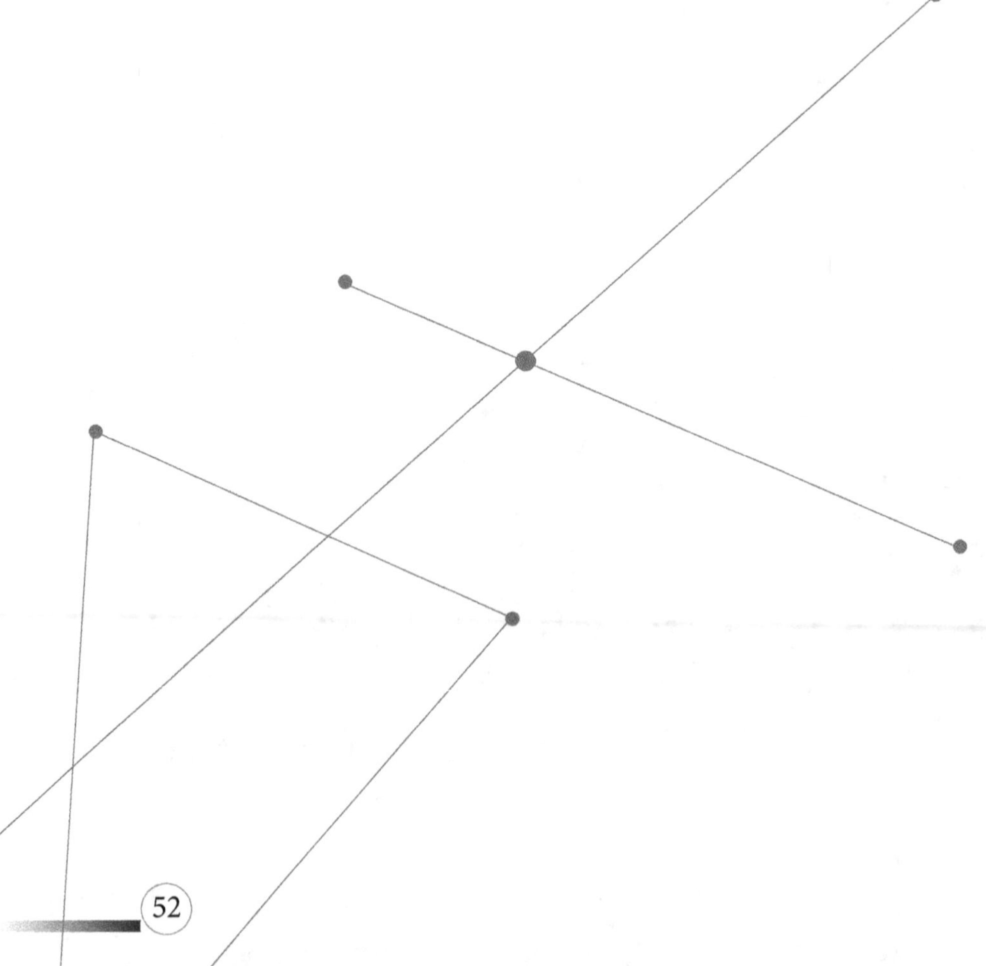

"Solar energy is also a guarantee of world peace and will impact the new geopolitics. No one will have to wage new wars to have access to the energy resources of other nations. And the sun is present in all countries and is a heritage for public use"

Henderson Colina

Solar energy as a human right

We understand Human Rights as the set of prerogatives based on human dignity, whose effective realization is essential for the integral development of the person. Based on this principle, solar energy meets all the characteristics for its inclusion in the global list of inherent rights of the human being.

Achieving this recognition would significantly improve the quality of life of millions of people around the world, facilitate the implementation of global objectives to reduce the impacts that lead to climate change, promote greater economic prosperity, strengthen environmental education for the population in general. I would urge the governments of the planet in a determined way, to promote renewable energies for the common future.

Understanding that the sun has been present throughout the evolution of life and its constant evolutionary processes, that it is present at this moment and will continue to be present for future generations, has been the central approach during my research.

Understanding that the scientific and spiritual are two approaches that have tried to be separated, but in reality, not as absolute truth, have a very strong link. We see this reflected in: ancestral ways of life; their cultures; developed technologies; and in their spiritual manifestations of worship and adoration. Appreciating that in many of these reflections that the sun is present.

The sun is a form of energy that regenerates daily. Many cycles are linked to it. It is a form of recognition of the presence of light, clarity, understanding, to which is added that in many countries there are health methods that incorporate the use of sunlight for healing processes. For this reason, I believe that success surrounds companies since they have a prospective vision: the businessmen who bet decades ago on photovoltaic solar energy, constitutes a sample of a generation of advanced young people who deserve all our support and have earned our respect.

*"Global recognition
of the right to a healthy
environment will support
all efforts to leave no
one behind, ensuring
a fair transition to an
environmentally healthy and
socially equitable world, and
make human rights a reality
for all"*

**Joint declaration of United Nations entities on the right to
a healthy environment. Human Rights Council, 46th period of
sessions. General debate, point 32021.**

In 2015, the United Nations Organization announced the 17 Sustainable Development Goals for a common future. For this, world leaders adopted a set of global objectives to eradicate poverty, protecting the planet and ensuring prosperity for all as part of a new sustainable development agenda.

Most of these Global Objectives are closely related to the fact of undertaking actions in the area of renewable energies and respond to the legal instruments of international law for the respect and promotion of Human Rights for which the strengthening of alliances will be strategic and primordial.

There are some valuable antecedents in the efforts and initiatives undertaken by international organizations, academics and environmental associations to achieve the recognition of renewable energy as a legitimate Human Right.

In November 2005, during the World Renewable Energy Assembly and the 3rd World Renewable Energy Forum, events held in Bonn, Germany, the attendees stated in their final declaration, among others, that: "All human beings are born equal in dignity and rights".

This first article of the Universal Declaration of Human Rights articulates a basic commitment. Only by respecting this commitment you can secure a human life in peace. Energy is the fundamental prerequisite of every human life. The availability of energy is a fundamental and indivisible Human Right.

In November 2018 at the Eneref Institute, of Pennsylvania The United States proposed to the Office of the High Commissioner for Human Rights of the United Nations Organization that the Natural Light of the Interior (NID) be considered as a Human Right, since it would allow reducing the high energy consumption in the infrastructure, managing to impact in new construction models with ecological architecture that would allow greater access to sunlight with the positive implications that this has for human health and the well-being of the planet.

In the Rio Declaration, Brazil, a Precautionary principle was established: "In order to protect the environment, the States must widely apply the precautionary criterion according to their capacities. Where there is a danger of serious or irreversible damage, lack of full scientific certainty should not be used as a reason for postponing cost-effective measures to prevent environmental degradation."

According to this principle, the absence of practical evidence of potential damage is not a valid reason for not establishing the rules that are considered necessary to prevent the occurrence of harmful results. The In Dubio Pronatura, as a precautionary principle of prevention of Nature, is presented in order to enforce the laws and regulations that give us legitimate rights to protect and defend Mother Earth and cultural heritage-creating mechanisms that facilitate the enjoyment of a healthy and ecologically balanced life, as and access to various forms of environmental sustainability, including renewable energies.

We often see climatic events set new records. They occur unexpectedly at a speed that prevents modern response systems from offering the possibility of saving human lives and preventing the loss of other forms of life. Over the past year, various countries have been seriously affected by increasingly intense floods, hurricanes and tornadoes that are causing loss of life.

"We have already achieved the recognition of our human rights to water, clean air, healthy and pollution-free land, the time has come to recognize sunlight as a universal right of peoples, it is a form of inspiration for the new beginning in the era of renewable energies"

Henderson Colina

These natural disaster impact the economy and exacerbate the effects of the post-pandemic crisis, as well as the forced mobilization of families to new residential areas and the complete loss of their homes, increasing the number of climate refugees.

In this spirit, the United Nations Convention on Climate Change and its associated bodies have generated various declarations recognizing the need for access to renewable energy sources as a mechanism capable of slowing down the advance of high-impact climatic phenomena. In doing so they have elevated the concept of human rights into high-level debates on climate issues.

For its part, the United Nations Convention for the Protection of Human Rights, at the meetings of the Human Rights Council and the Office of the High Commissioner for Human Rights, have raised with the signatory countries and the general public that issues related to Climate Change must be considered from the perspective of fundamental rights, since they put at risk the durability of human life, peace, health and other genuine rights inherent to global society.

Likewise, other global legal instruments give us a basis for the proposal: The Universal Declaration of Human Rights (UDHR) of 1945 refers to the adequate standard of living that ensures people's health, food and housing, among other elements. In the Universal Declaration of Emerging Human Rights (DUDHE), a programmatic instrument of civil society that emerged from the celebration of the Universal Forum of Cultures in Barcelona (2004), expressly highlights "the right of every human being to have access to drinking water, sanitation and energy".

The International Covenant on Economic, Social and Cultural Rights (ICESCR) of 1966, recognizes in its article 11 the right to adequate housing, which includes aspects related to access to energy for cooking, lighting and heating.

The Convention on the Elimination of all forms of Discrimination against Women (CEDEM) of 1979, in article 14, point "h", urges the States parties to adopt measures to eliminate discrimination against women, pointing out among them the of "Enjoying adequate living conditions, particularly in the areas of housing, health services, electricity and water supply, transportation and communications".

In addition, the right to energy is part of the typified elements as conditions of the right to adequate housing, established in the General Comment No. 4 of the United Nations of 1991. In particular, regarding the availability of services, materials, facilities and infrastructure, affordability and habitability.

It is also important to remember that human rights are universal legal guarantees that protect individuals and groups, not only from actions, but also from omissions that interfere with their freedoms and fundamental rights, a concept that evolves according to what each era society considers "human dignity".

This effort to achieve the recognition of solar energy as a universal heritage for the peoples of the world, is then a binding right to which everyone would have access and the governments of the world must facilitate access to technologies derived from the sun.

I firmly believe then that: The time has come to materialize the principle that the sun rises for all as a premise of equality, ensuring that the peoples of the planet have access to solar energy as a legitimate right that was granted to us by Life. This is a technology that is easy to install and has a low economic cost. It is also a source that allows families energy independence and an immediate response to reducing their carbon footprint.

> *"The time has come to materialize the egalitarian premise that the Sun rises for everyone"*
>
> **Henderson Colina**

Despite all this, it is necessary that the legal frameworks are established for the development and regulation of renewable energies, which must be a public service in which free competition and private initiative are possible together with the reduction of costs and clear regulation. In the South American continent, various laws have been developed in search of efficiency and energy planning.

Many of these the solar energy production sectors have been incorporated as one of the most important items within renewable energies. Countries such as Brazil, Chile, Colombia, Costa Rica, Ecuador, Mexico, Nicaragua, Panama, Peru, Uruguay and Venezuela have legal instruments in favor of renewable energy and energy efficiency. They are only expected to be executed.

On the subject of renewable energy, the United Nations Organization (UN), the World Bank (WB) or the World Trade Organization (WTO) try to homogenize the regulations of renewable energies and sustainable development in the international order. This issue is led from the environmental point of view through renewable energy and sustainable economic development. Have been developed international legal instruments on their basis such as the United Nations Framework Convention on Climate Change and the Kyoto Protocol. These legal frameworks have been allowed to be incorporated into internal establishments.

These legal frameworks have allowed to be incorporated into their internal estate, in each country this responds to the environmental agenda, leaving the responsibility to the ministries with competence in the environmental and energy area, it is very varied, in some Nations, the energy issue is united to the environmental issue and are managed as a single strategy, in others, they are separate agencies or ministries that respond to a country agenda, but sometimes they complicate and bureaucratize the initiatives, it is an issue that we have to address for each region of the planet. For its part, Chile has incorporated since 1997, 10 regulations and two laws referring to the energy issue, of which 4 are specific for renewable energies that involve solar thermal systems.

Most countries constitutions have advanced towards the recognition of the Human Rights of the population. Likewise, they have created legal mechanisms that facilitate access to energy. In some cases, renewable energies are cited as a sector capable of guaranteeing energy independence, all seen from a geopolitical perspective of self-determination to reduce dependence on oil and other conventional forms of energy.

This is a great advance, however what we are proposing here is the premise of recognizing the solar energy source as a genuine right, which is already a reality. And raising it to the world political debate, as a sign of humanitarian awareness and a manifestation of respect for other forms of life present on our planet.

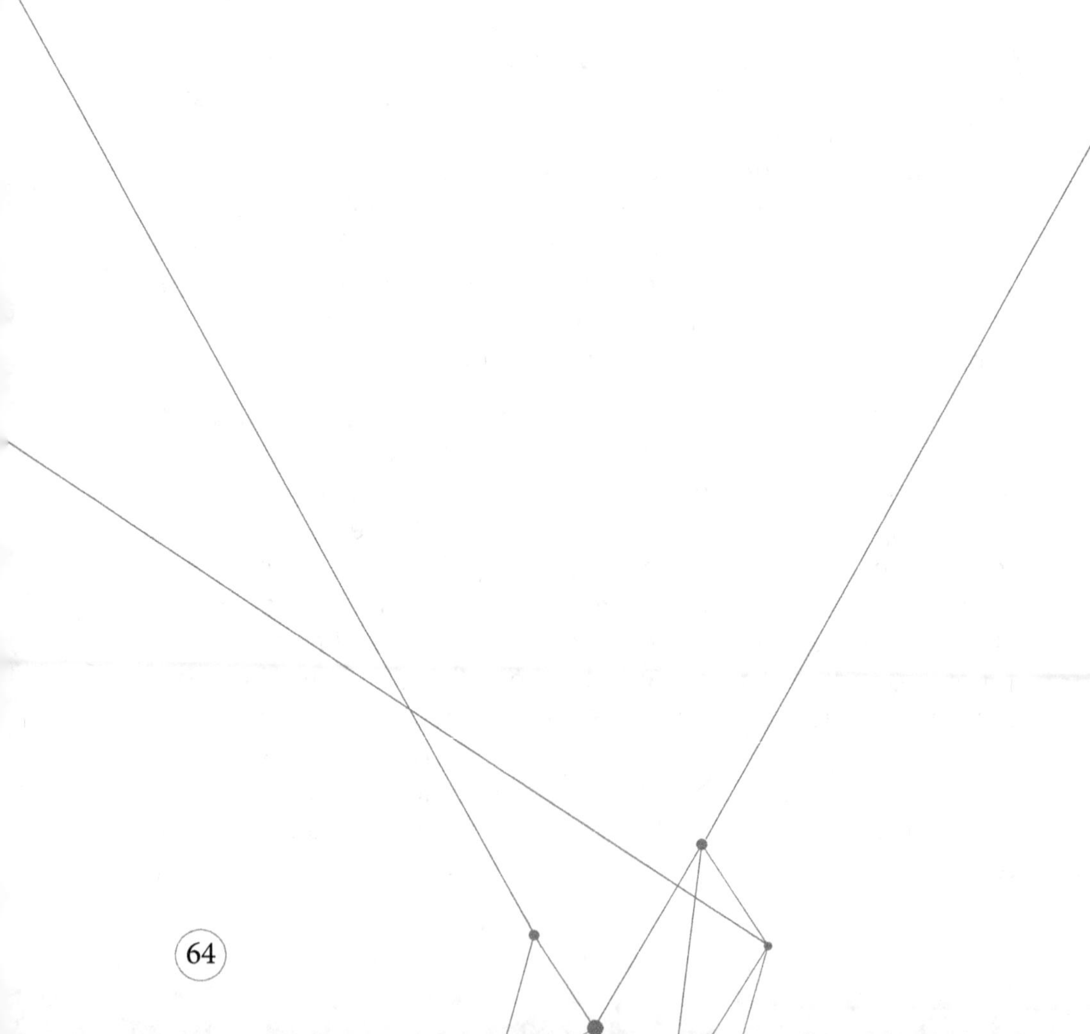

Environmental education, key to promote solar energy

When I became an environmental educator I learned this principle: "nobody loves what they don't know". Most of the world's problems are associated with ignorance and lack of love, so the best way to move forward on this renewable energy issue is to massively inform and educate the population. Sometimes we notice resistance due to ignorance.

My recommendation for all renewable energy companies and corporations, and especially for solar energy companies, is to "create environmental education programs, this will make it easier for the majority of the population to be aware and there will no longer be a need to knock on the doors of families to convince them to be solar, people will come to the offices, people will look for all the ways to get access to solar energy, because they will be informed and the information creates social empowerment".

In 2008, during the tenth Conference of the Parties to the RAMSAR Convention on Wetlands, I had the opportunity to visit the facilities of the Renewable Energy Center of the City of Changwon, in South Korea. There, the Hyundai Company presented one of its first hybrid-solar car models. At that time it seemed unlikely to materialize the common use of this technology. Currently there are several proposals, one of the most consolidated and viable is the one presented by the Tesla Corporation.

During the last decades we have observed how climatic events have intensified generating serious impacts on a global scale: massive migratory processes, violent and surprising floods, hurricanes or increasingly powerful tornadoes, accelerating the loss and modification of ecosystems and populations.

Some nations of the planet have undertaken actions through the various International Organizations, which have resulted in initiatives that have allowed the restoration of ecosystems, the protection of natural areas and strengthened environmental education, however, a structural change must still be generated. Since the dependence on conventional energies is still in force, keeping the carbon footprint as the main responsible for global changes. The association between Environmental Education and Renewable Energies is important.

Around the world there are already many organizations addressing these issues. Renewable energy education is a model that promotes the development of attitudes and values that incorporate non-conventional renewable sources of energy. This is based on the works of Broman 1984, which includes the didactic approach that is dynamized with the knowledge of objects, where it is sought to incorporate means and devices that allow you to interact with technology and understand its operation. An example of this could be seen by taking cars with rechargeable solar panel technology to schools, as well as trucks and buses transformed into laboratories or internal centers that allow children, young people and adults to interact within a thematic space in which it is possible create a museum not only of the objects but also with the environment.

A renewable energy program must be accompanied by trained personnel at different levels of training, this can be the basis for its success with a design that allows addressing various issues with a transversal axis of knowledge. It is important to understand that it is possible to create an environmental education model on renewable energies including the characteristics, types, uses, benefits, potential and restrictions of solar energy.

From this it is possible to develop a map of the community's knowledge in order to develop attitudes, values, interests and behaviors around the subject.

Around the planet there are already various initiatives to promote the strengthening of capacities in renewable energies with an emphasis on photovoltaic solar energy, since it is the technology that leads this sector. Some Universities and Centers for Higher Professional Studies offer programs, courses and specializations in green energy and it can be seen that solar energy occupies an important place in most of the content in said training.

The 4 goals of education for solar energy

The goals of solar energy education are to provide functional knowledge and generate an understanding of facts, concepts, principles, and technologies of solar energy sources. Depending on the level, the role of education in renewable energies should be, in addition to educational: informative, investigative and imaginative. Specific goals of an education program may include:

Already since 1978 a lab studies plan for the teaching of alternative and renewable energy sources was developed within the high school industrial arts laboratory at Montclair State College in New Jersey, USA. Like this, other groups around the world have developed programs and school packages.

Mary Powell, from Sunrun, in the United States, stated during an interview conducted by the New York Times that "A house with solar panels, for example, will use as much clean energy as it needs and then it can send any extra in the house to the network so that clean energy can be used within the community where it was produced.

Develop awareness of the nature and causes of energy-related problems facing humanity, such as scarcity, rising prices of fossil fuel prices, climate change, energy equity and availability among others.

Raise awareness about the energy issue by disseminating knowledge and skills about renewable energy sources such as solar energy, showing it's potential, existing technology, the cost-price relationship with personal and environmental health, and the benefit to society.

Motivate on the development and implementation of alternative strategies to face the various problems of the energy sector, such as solar energy to meet the growing global energy requirements in an environmentally sustainable manner.

Develop functional values and attitudes for the use of solar energy sources and the associated socioeconomic and environmental dimensions.

Now that storage is combined with solar energy, it is possible to return energy to the grid only when it is most needed and valuable", this is a way of raising public awareness about the response capacity of the renewable energy sector.

Now, if we manage to systematize it in a pedagogical way and educate children and young people in schools and the general public through microphones on radio and television networks, as well as all the forms that information technologies offer us and communication including social networks and the next digital meta universes, we will win more solar allies for the future.

The world of Culture is also making its important contributions. A significant number of museums and cultural study centers around the planet already maintain permanent exhibitions on renewable energy, emphasizing the contribution and high impact of the various forms of solar energy, especially photovoltaic solar energy. Also, many buildings in the global culture network are installing solar panels on their infrastructure.

Since 1994, the United Nations Educational, Scientific and Cultural Organization (UNESCO) undertook a process leading to a World Solar Energy Summit and the World Solar Energy Program project 1996-2005.

The World Solar Energy Program is an open attempt through foreign partnerships and cooperation's between governments and organizations to encourage the adoption, the widest possible use of renewable energy sources and energy conservation. Similarly, UNESCO has valued the incorporation of renewable energy sources in World Heritage sites, recognizing that Climate Change represents a threat to Humanity and therefore to the entire global network of sites that have been declared of exceptional value for our culture and identity.

I can see a fleet of cars with solar panels arriving at schools and communities showing all our people the benefits, profitability and viability of photovoltaic solar energy, the development of school scientific events, art fairs, and contests for children and young people.

A whole set of actions promoted by environmental education programs from companies and governments, this is possible.

I would like the green corporations to assume the creation of departments on technological innovation and environmental education, the formation of human capital is the key. In addition to maintaining motivation, knowing and exchanging the various experiences in other regions and countries, the socialization of knowledge through associations that bring together the business community and social investment by large corporations as mechanisms to facilitate access to solar energy.

The revision of the educational system has allowed us to reflect on the need for a more experiential education. These processes help perception and learning through cognitive methods that will allow the inclusion of all.

The great education campaigns in public places, airports, the continuous publication of books, virtual editions, television microphones, the use of social networks and all the communication potential of this era, are imperative. It's the moment. I am sure that in the contemporary history of humanity we will be remembered as the generation that made solar energy possible as a global right, for justice, peace and love among all, I have no doubt about it.

"And Solar Energy reached everyone and the warriors of light will be remembered as the generation that left an indelible mark on us: that of green technology that of love for the planet, leaving behind what humanity once called the footprint of carbon".

Thanks

REFERENCES

1. Arwood, J. W. (1997). Institutionalizing solar energy education (No. CONF-970441-). American Solar Energy Society, Boulder, CO (United States).

2. Álvaro López Peña (2016), Las renovables ya no son caras, y no solo mejoran el medio ambiente, también la economía, tomado de: https://www.consumer.es/medioambiente/alvaro-lopez-pena-agencia-internacional-de-las-energias-renovables-irena.html.

3. Algarín, C.R., Llanos, A.P., & Castro, A.O. (2017). An analytic hierarchy process based approach for evaluating renewable energy sources. International Journal of Energy Economics and Policy, 7(4), 38-47.

4. Robles-Algarín, C. A., Taborda-Giraldo, J. A., & Ospino-Castro, A. J. (2018). Procedimiento para la Selección de Criterios en la Planificación Energética de Zonas Rurales Colombianas. Información tecnológica, 29(3), 71-80.

5. Algarin, C. R., & Álvarez, O. R. (2018). Un panorama de las energías renovables en el Mundo, Latinoamérica y Colombia. Espacios, 39(34), 10.

6. A. Einstein, On the quantum theory of radiation. Physikalische Zeitschrift 18 (1917)

7. Banco Interamericano de Desarrollo (BID). (2015). Integración de las energías renovables no convencionales en Colombia, 370p.

8. Ballesteros-Ballesteros, V. A., & Gallego-Torres, A. P. (2019). Modelo de educación en energías renovables desde el compromiso público y la actitud energética. Revista Facultad de Ingeniería, 28(52), 27-42.

9. Becquerel, A. E. (1839). Recherches sur les effets de la radiation chimique de la lumiere solaire au moyen des courants electriques. CR Acad. Sci, 9(145), 1.

10. Bonilla, C. S., & Cordero, J. M. (2019). La dimensión jurídica de la energía eléctrica y las energías renovables en México. Rev. Digital de Derecho Admin., 22, 299.

11. Brock, A., Sovacool, B. K., & Hook, A. (2020). Volatile Photovoltaics: Green Industrialization, Sacrifice Zones, and the Political Ecology of Solar Energy in Germany. Annals of the American Association of Geographers, 1-23.

12. Brundtland, G. H. (1987). Informe de la Comisión Mundial sobre el Medio Ambiente y el Desarrollo: Nuestro futuro común. Documentos de Las Naciones Unidas. 416.

13. Chapin, D. M., Fuller, C. S., & Pearson, G. L. (1954). A new silicon p-n junction photocell for converting solar radiation into electrical power. Journal of Applied Physics, 25(5), 676-677.

14. Corporación Andina de Fomento (CAF) (2012). Green Climate Fund. Programa Energia Solar – Venezuela.

15. Dan D'Ambrosio Burlington Free Press (2021). Mary Powell named CEO of San Francisco-based solar installation company Sunrun.

16. De Winter, F. (1986). Economic and Policy Aspects of Solar Energy. In Intersol Eighty Five (pp. 2207-2218). Pergamon.

17. Dolter, B. D., & Boucher, M. (2018). Solar energy justice: A case-study analysis of Saskatchewan, Canada. Applied Energy, 225, 221-232.

18. E. Becquerel, Mémoire sur les effets électriques produits sous l'influence des rayons solaires. Comptes Rendus 9, 561–567 (Issue date: 7 May 1935) (1839)

19. Esborraz, D. (2016). El Modelo Ecológico Alternativo Latinoamericanoentre Protección Del Derecho Humano Al Medio Ambiente Y Reconocimiento De Los Derechos De La Naturalize (The Latin-American Alternative Ecological Model between the Protection of the Environment as a Human Right and the Recognition of the Rights of Nature). Revista Derecho del Estado, (36).

20. Eneref Institute PR for Planet Earth (2018). Right to Daylight Letter to High Commissioner Bachelet.

21. Faunce, T. (2012). Governing planetary nanomedicine: environmental sustainability and a UNESCO universal declaration on the bioethics and human rights of natural and artificial photosynthesis (global solar fuels and foods). Nanoethics, 6(1), 15-27.

22. Fraas, L. M. (2014). Low-cost solar electric power (pp. 31-42). New York: Springer.

23. Glazebrook, S. (2009). Human rights and the environment. Victoria U. Wellington L. Rev., 40, 293.

24. Global Witness (2021). Land and environmental defenders: annual report archive.

25. Gilson, S. C., & Abbott, S. (2017). Tesla Motors (B): Merging with SolarCity. Tesla Motors (B): Merging with Solarcity." Harvard Business School case study (218-038).

26. Harvad University. What CEOS Say (2019). Webcast with Mary Powell, President and CEO of Green Mountain Power. https://www.hsph.harvard.edu/leadership-studio/what-ceos-say/mary-powell.

27. Handl, G. (2012). Declaration of the United Nations conference on the human environment (Stockholm Declaration), 1972 and the Rio Declaration on Environment and Development, 1992. United Nations Audiovisual Library of International Law, 11.

28. Hasnain, S. M., Alawaji, S. H., & Elani, U. A. (1998). Solar energy education-a viable pathway for sustainable development. Renewable Energy, 14(1-4), 387-392.

29. IRENA, Renewable Energy Benefits Leveraging Local Capacity For Solar PV, (2017). https://www.irena.org//media/Files/IRENA/Agency/Publication/2017/Jun/IRENA_Leveraging_for_Solar_PV_2017.pdf.

30. IRENA, International Renewable Energy Agency Renewable Capacity Statistics (2019). https://www.irena.org//media/Files/IRENA/Agency/Publication/2019/Mar/IRENA_RE_Capacity_Statistics_2019.pdf.

31. IRENA, REmap 2030, A renewable energy roadmap, summary of findings, Spanish (2014). https://www.irena.org/-/media/Files/IRENA/Agency/Publication/2014/IRENA_REmap_2030_summary_2014_ES.PDF?la=en&hash=48A69749036ED8753C92FD5F-4951C79C01CD1F1F.

32. IRENA, "Renewable power generation costs in 2020" ISBN: 978-92-9260-348-9" (2021) https://www.irena.org/- /media/Files/IRENA/Agency/Publication/2021/Jun/IRENA_Power_Generation_Costs_2020_hig   hlights_ES.pdf?la=en&hash=7167169864B153 0F3947D1F6E5BB32260A93B4FB

33. IRENA (2021) & International Labour Organization. Renewable Energy and Jobs Annual Review 2021.

34. J. Russo y R.O. Russo. (2009) In dubio pro natura: un principio de precaución y prevención a favor de los recursos naturales. Tierra Tropical, 1(1), 23-32.

35. Jolly, S. (2014). Application of solar energy in South Asia: promoting intergenerational equity in climate law and policy. International Journal of Private Law, 7(1), 20-39.

36. Jones, G. G., & Bouamane, L. (2012). " Power from Sunshine": A Business History of Solar Energy. Harvard Business School Working Paper Series.

37. Júnior, C. L., Rodrigues, B. B., Silva, F. V. V., Luz, L. R., & de Aguiar Lima, R. L. F. (2018). Energia solar: metodologia para avaliação do local de instalação de sistema fotovoltaico fomentando a educação ambiental. Revista Brasileira de Educação Ambiental (RevBEA), 13(3), 233-244.

38. Kopnina, H. (2015). Sustainability in environmental education: new strategic thinking. Environment, development and sustainability, 17(5), 987-1002.

39. Kim, H. (2020). Analysis of How Tesla Creates Core Innovation Capability. International Journal of Business and Management, 15(6), 42-61.

40. Kudachimath, BS y Ragashetti, NS (2015). Innovación disruptiva: cómo Tesla Motors, SpaceX y Solar City están revolucionando las industrias. Revista internacional de gestión, TI e ingeniería , 5 (8), 109-117.

41. T. C. Kandpal, and L. Broman (2016) Renewable Energy Education for the Future. Sweden: Strömstad Akademi.

42. The New York Times. ENERGY & ENVIROMENT (2021). "A Rooftop Solar Company Hires a Utility Veteran as Chief Executive", By Evan Penn. https://www.nytimes.com/2021/08/05/business/energy-environment/sunrun-mary-powell-ceo.html.

43. Thorme, M. (1990). Establishing environment as a human right. Denv. J. Int'l L. & Pol'y, 19, 301.

44. Tsoutsos, T., Frantzeskaki, N., & Gekas, V. (2005). Environmental impacts from the solar energy technologies. Energy policy, 33(3), 289-296.

45. L. Broman, and A. Ott, (1988) "Solar education: the way forward," Sun at Work in Europe, vol. 6, pp. 24-25.

46. Londoño-Parra, C. M., & Ramírez-Echavarría, J. L. (2013). Normas de eficiencia energética de motores de inducción,¿ está preparada Latinoamérica?. TecnoLógicas, (30), 117-147.

47. Lovelock, J., & Margulis, L. (2007). The gaia hypothesis. New York.

48. Lovelock, J. E., & Rioja, A. J. (1983). Gaia: una nueva visión de la vida sobre la tierra. Madrid: Hermann Blume.

49. Margulis, L., 1971. Symbiosis and Evolution. Scientific American. 225: 48-57.

50. Margulis, L. (1998) Symbiotic Planet: A New Look At Evolution.

51. Margulis, L; & Sagan D (2000). What Is Life?.

52. Matthews, T., Hirve, M., Pan, Y., Dang, D., Rawar, E., & Daim, T. U. (2020). Tesla Energy. In Innovation Management in the Intelligent World (pp. 233-249). Springer, Cham.

53. Meadows, D. H., Meadows, D. L., Randers, J., & Behrens, W. W. (1972). Los límites del crecimiento: informe al Club de Roma sobre el predicamento de la humanidad.

54. Morse, R. N. (1977). Solar energy in Australia. Ambio, 209-215.

55. Moula, M. E. (2014). Right to know: Solar Panel in Bangladesh. Energy bangla, www-energybangla.

56. McClymonds, J. T. (1992). Human Right to a Healthy Environment: An International Legal Perspective, The. NYL Sch. L. Rev., 37, 583.

57. National Governors Association USA (2017). Summer Meeting Report.

58. Navarro Veguillas, L. (2000). Contribuciones de Einstein a la teoría cuántica (1905-1925). Arbor, 2000, vol. 167, núm. 659-660, p. 437-457.

59. The RAMSAR Convention (2008). COP10 delegates report, Changwon City, Korea.

60. RRA, Evaluaciones de preparación de energías renovables (2021), https://www.irena.org/rra Atlas Global, Energía Renovable, 2021, https://irena.org/globalatlas.

61. Rose, H. (1982). Solar Energy Now. Ann Arbor Science Publishers, 230 Collingwood, PO Box 1425, Ann Arbor, Michigan 48106.

62. Sachs, W. (2004). Environment and human rights. Development, 47(1), 42-49.

63. Saylan, C., & Blumstein, D. (2011). The failure of environmental education (and how we can fix it). University of California Press.

64. Sengupta, M., Habte, A., Wilbert, S., Gueymard, C., & Remund, J. (2021). Best practices handbook for the collection and use of solar resource data for solar energy applications (No. NREL/TP-5D00-77635). National Renewable Energy Lab.(NREL), Golden, CO (United States).

65. Sigüenza, F. R. (2019). Tendencias globales de las energías renovables: las energías solar y eólica se convierten en las tecnologías de generación con mayor atractivo de inversión. Cuadernos de energía, (58), 57-75

66. Shelton, D. (1991). Human rights, environmental rights, and the right to environment. Stan. j. Int'l L., 28, 103.

67. Stupnitska, N. I., & Sribna, E. V. (2016). Historical Aspects Of Solar Energy In The World. In Economics, Management, Law: Problems Of Establishing And Transformation (pp. 33-35).

68. Sulaiman, S. N. (2011). Educação ambiental, sustentabilidade e ciência: o papel da mídia na difusão de conhecimentos científicos. Ciência & Educação (Bauru), 17, 645-662.

69. SUNRUN (2020). The Future of Energy is More Exciting Than You Think, by Mary Powell, CEO of Sunrun.

70. National Geographic Society (2019) Theory of Evolution. Subjects Biology, Ecology, Earth Science, Geology, Geography, Physical Geography. Grades 5-8.

71. US Department of Energy (2021). Solar Energy Evolution and Diffusion Studies (SEEDS) Solar Energy Technologies Office

72. United Nations (1992). La Conferencia de las Naciones Unidas sobre el Medio Ambiente y el Desarrollo. Declaración de Rio de Janeiro sobre el Medio Ambiente y Desarrollo.

73. United Nations (2015). The Global Goals for Sustainable Development.

74. United Nations (2018). Los efectos de lento inicio del cambio climático y la protección de los derechos humanos de los migrantes transfronterizos.

75. United Nations (2020), The Promise of Solar Power: Energy Strategy to Reduce Carbon Emissions in the 21st Century. https://www.un.org/en/chronicle/article/promise-solar-energy-low-carbon-energy-strategy-21st-century.

76. United Nations (2020). Estudio analítico sobre la promoción y protección de los derechos de las personas con discapacidad en el contexto del cambio climático.

77. United Nations (2021). Joint statement of United Nations entities on the right to healthy environment.

78. United Nations (2021), UN chief calls for 'urgent transition' from fossil fuels to renewable energy. https://news.un.org/en/story/2021/01/1081802.

79. United Nations (2021), Solar energy, renewable and profitable. https://news.un.org/es/story/2018/04/1430451.

80. United Nations (2021). Resolución 217 A (III) de 1948 Declaración Universal de Derechos Humanos.

81. United Nations (2021). resolución 2200 A (XXI), de 1966. Pacto Internacional de Derechos Económicos, Sociales y Culturales.

82. United Nations (2021). Asamblea General en su resolución 34/180 de 1979. Convención sobre la eliminación de todas las formas de discriminación contra la mujer.

83. United Nations (2021). Oficina del Alto Comisionado de Derechos Humanos. El derecho a una vivienda adecuada (Art.11, párr. 1): 13/12/91.

84. United Nations (2021). A study on promoting and protecting the rights of older people from the effects of climate change.

85. United Nations (2021). Convención Marco de las Naciones Unidas sobre el Cambio Climático, aprobada en 1994.

86. United Nations (2021). Protocolo de Kyoto, aprobado el 11 de diciembre de 1997.

87. United Nations (2021). Enmienda de Doha al Protocolo de Kyoto aprobada el 8 de diciembre de 2012.

88. UNESCO (1994). World Solar Programme (WSP).

89. UNESCO (2021). Renewable Energy Transition and World Heritage.

90. World Council for Renewable Energy (2005). For the human right to renewable energy. World Council for Renewable Energy. https://www.wcre.org/index.php.

91. W.G. Adams, R.E. Day, The action of light on selenium. Proc R Soc A25, 113 (1877).

92. Zaman, R., van Vliet, O., & Posch, A. (2021). Energy access and pandemic-resilient livelihoods: The role of solar energy safety nets. Energy Research & Social Science, 71.

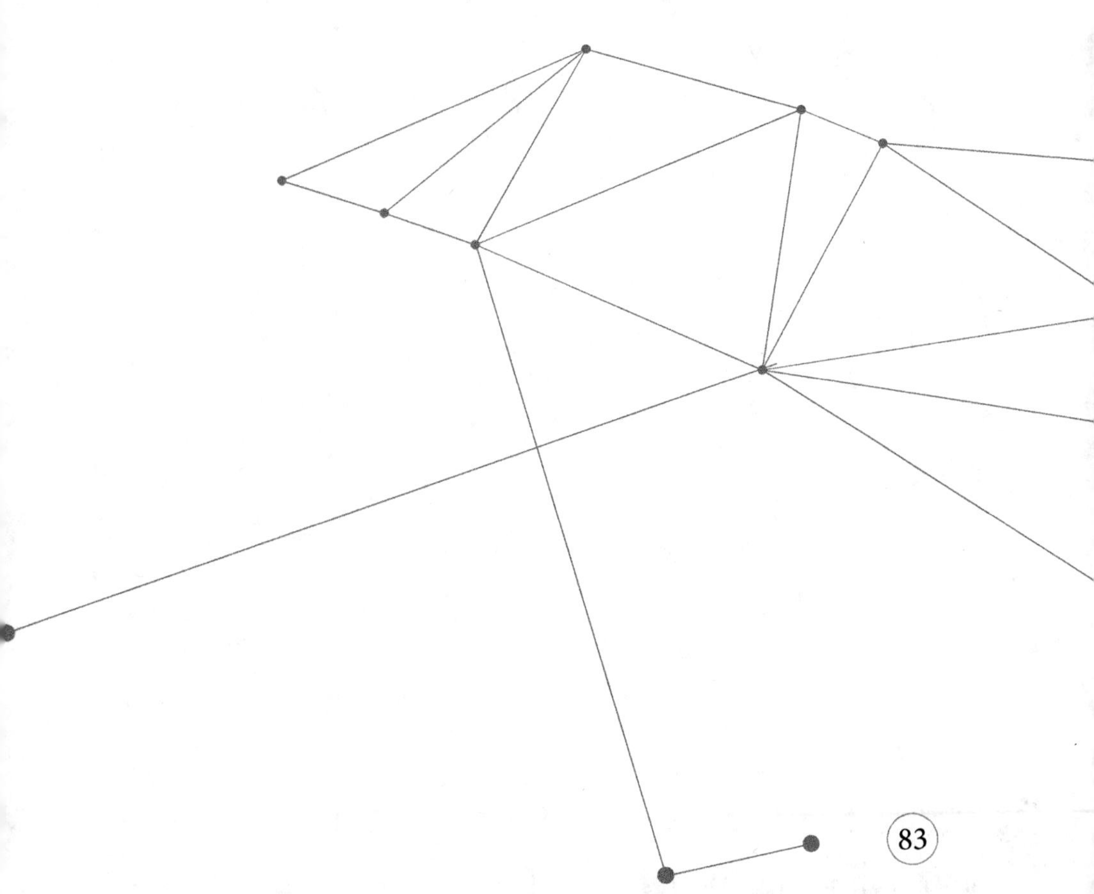